Waiting on God

A 4 Week Advent Devotional
with Journaling and Conversation
Prompts
By Renee Davis Meyer

Advent is a season of
waiting:
What are we waiting for?

1

It seems like I should dedicate this to my sweet family, but the truth is:
This is for my Selah Sisters. You know who you are.

Waiting on God: A 4 Week Advent
Devotional with Journaling and conversation prompts
By Renee Davis Meyer

Find Bible Studies, Devotionals & Encouragement from Renee Davis Meyer at ReeMeyer.com

I am so glad you've decided to go on this Advent journey!

Advent is a season of waiting: What are we waiting for? Over the next 25 days we will answer that question, diving deep into the Biblical concept of waiting on God. I love these Scriptures—culled from a list of every mention of Waiting on God in the Bible—and I hope you'll learn to love them as well.

I am blessed, stretched, pushed, and encouraged by each aspect of waiting on God. Like a diamond, all of these facets combine to reveal great beauty. We have a God who is worth waiting on, and He has given Himself to us freely and fully. This is what we celebrate at Christmas: What a gift!

I don't want you to stop with my thoughts about these verses and Waiting on God, I want you to think your own thoughts. I hope this devotional opens up a conversation between you and God, about what waiting means for *you*.

With that in mind, after each reading and devotional, you will find 3 journaling prompts: Questions for you to think through, ways to process your own story, and prayer suggestions. You can work through all three journaling prompts each day if you have time, or pick and choose one that resonates most for you.

On the 7th day of each week you'll find a day set aside for extended journaling, extra time to process what you're learning about Advent and Waiting, or catching up on any missed days.

I find I grow more when I'm able to talk about what I'm learning. So the 7th day also includes community/family conversation starters, questions you can discuss with anyone, whether or not they are doing this Advent study with you.

I picture these discussions over lunch after church on Sundays, or while sharing a cup of coffee with friends, or gathered around the dinner table.

In our family, we have these conversations on Sundays nights, along with lighting a candle in our Advent Wreath.

Each seventh day also includes a quote from Andrew Murray, who published a little book called Waiting on

God in 1958. I found a copy in a used bookstore as a young believer and it has shaped my thinking and my life since then. I couldn't write about waiting on God without acknowledging Murray's influence on my thinking, and sharing some of his actual words with you. I've tried to force it on many fellow readers and seekers over the years, but most found his language too dated to handle in large chunks. I love it. If you'd like to give it a try, it's a public domain book so easily available on line, and for under $1 on Kindle.

A word about Devotionals

This study of Waiting on God is divided into daily readings over the 25 days between December 1 and 25th. Advent devotionals have been a part of my spiritual practice many Decembers now, so I have some advice for this devotional or any other you pick up.

For me the KEY to sticking with any Advent practice, rather than giving up 3 days or 2 weeks in: If you miss reading a day, just skip it. If you miss 3 days, skip three days. Whenever you have time to read again, read that date's devotional. Don't think about it in terms of "getting behind." You can always go back and catch up on past ones if you have time. But each day, start with today.

Good advice for advent devotionals and for life: Every day, be where you are.

Set aside time and space, daily when possible, in this (needlessly) crazy season, but don't stress if you miss a day. When you can, say no to something else so that you can say yes to time for your soul. Say yes to time this Advent Season to breathe, pray, and lift your eyes to the God who created and loves you.

Lingering long on the idea of Waiting on God has been a treasure to me. I am so excited for you to discover it too.

You are my hiding place and my shield; I wait for Your Word. (Psalm 119:114)

Welcome to the Waiting

December 1

But as for me, I will watch expectantly for the Lord; I will wait for the God of my salvation. My God will hear me. (Micah 7:7)

Merriam-Webster.com offers several definitions for the word *wait:* To stay in place, in expectation or readiness (wait your turn, waiting for a train.) To look forward expectantly (waiting to see what will happen, waiting to strike.) To be ready and available (slippers waiting by the bed.) To serve at meals (waiting tables.)

In the Christian Church calendar, Advent is the season of waiting. During advent, we remember the world's long wait for the promised Messiah, and we join the ancient mothers and fathers of our faith, waiting on God. Like patients in a waiting room, we wait for God to answer our prayers. Like people waiting for a train, we wait for Jesus to finish what He started when He entered the world two centuries ago. We wait expectantly for Him to keep His promises. Though we'd hardly say it out loud, in many ways we're waiting for God to do what we want Him to do. Hopefully we're waiting like slippers by the bed, ready and available to the Lord, and like a waiter, ready to serve Him and His people.

In the New Testament, Hebrews 11 includes a beautiful description of Old Testament saints who believed God's promises, even though they died without seeing those promises fulfilled.

All these died in faith, without receiving the promises, but having seen them and having welcomed them from a distance, and having confessed that they were strangers and exiles on the earth. (Hebrews 11:13)

I find myself loathe to practice waiting well. I don't like being delayed in traffic. Waiting for my kids to find their shoes makes me crazy. I'm irritated when Amazon Prime can't get my purchases to me in the promised 2 days.

And when I face the need for spiritual endurance, when answered prayers are delayed, when I serve faithfully and don't get the results I crave, I am tempted to give up or move on. The particular stream of American Christianity I find myself in hasn't really taught me to welcome God's promises from a distance.

I want to learn to wait well. I want to embrace a posture of patience, first with God and second with others and myself. I want to submit myself to the saints of old, and learn what it means to wait on the Lord.

This Advent season, will you practice waiting with me? Look for opportunities for patience. Welcome delayed and unanswered prayers. Lean into the promises of God, even those we might not see fulfilled until the fullness of time.

Watch expectantly for the Lord, who does hear us. Maybe we'll be surprised to find what we're really waiting for.

Journaling Prompts:

Which definition of waiting resonates the most with where you are now? Why?

What is your hope this Advent season? What do you want from God, what are you waiting for?

Write out a prayer, expressing your hopes for this month and season. Tell the Lord what you're afraid of, what you're excited about, and what you'd like to get out of the time you've set aside to think about waiting on Him.

Waiting on God in Silence

December 2

My soul waits in silence for God only; from Him is my salvation... Psalm 62:1

Historically Advent is a season of quiet. God's people wait in stillness for His arrival, His coming, God-With-Us. We often conclude the season of Advent singing of silent wonder. This is one of my favorite memories of Christmas: A quiet church with voices (and perhaps candles) raised, singing *"Silent Night, Holy Night, all is calm, all is bright."*

The irony of *that* song in what we've made of *this* season never fails to get my attention. Sometimes it is funny and sometimes heartbreaking. Silent Night, Holy Night? If I want any quiet at all during the Christmas season, I have to fight for it, and fight hard.

Christmas can be LOUD.

This is the season of noise and the season of lists: Things we want, things to buy, good deeds to do, gatherings to attend. December rings with the music of parties, the raised voices of maybe more family time than anyone needs, the strident call of all the obligations and expectations we put on ourselves. For some of us, this season is also loud with the wail of unspoken pain. Lost loved ones, lost hopes and dreams, loneliness.

What would it look like, in the midst of this loud season, to carve out some quiet for your soul?

Can you choose a regular daily time to step out of your lists, to turn off the noise, to take your pain or your joy and sit in silence with God?

Can you reserve some moments at the beginning or end of your day to sit with Jesus and wait? Perhaps over your lunch hour, or your littles' nap time?

There is a time for lists, for conversations, for requests. Jesus looked people in the eyes and asked, "What do you want me to do for you?" (Mark 10:51)

But there is also a time for silence, even with Jesus. What would it look like for you to sit with God as your friend, without requests or lists? Not asking for solutions or filling up the space with your words and thoughts. What does it look like to wait on God in silence?

Our souls need more quiet than this loud world provides.

Don't wait for Christmas Eve to enjoy a silent night, a silent moment. Set aside time to intentionally, purposefully wait on God, in silence.

My soul, wait in silence for God only, For my hope is from Him.

He only is my rock and my salvation, My stronghold; I shall not be shaken.

On God my salvation and my glory rest; The rock of my strength, my refuge is in God.

Trust in Him at all times, O people; Pour out your heart before Him; God is a refuge for us. Selah. (Psalm 62:5-8)

Journaling Prompts:

What feels loud in your life right now?

As you step into this advent season, what specific time have you set aside to be quiet, to be with Jesus and learn to wait on God?

Does the idea of sitting silently with God make you uncomfortable? Why or why not?

Waiting on God in Dependence

December 3

*They all wait for You To give them their food in due
season. You give to them, they gather it up;
You open Your hand, they are satisfied with good.
(Psalm 104:27-28)*

Psalm 104 is a celebration of God as Creator. The Psalmist
praises God while affirming His sovereign will over His
creation. "*The mountains rose; the valleys sank down to
the place which You established for them. You set a
boundary that they may not pass over, So that they will
not return to cover the earth...*"

Psalm 104 reminds us that the natural place of the
creature, the posture of all created things, is dependence.
Creation waits on the creator to provide.

O Lord, how many are Your works! In wisdom You have

made them all; The earth is full of Your possessions.

There is the sea, great and broad, In which are swarms without number, Animals both small and great...

They all wait for You To give them their food in due season. You give to them, they gather it up; You open Your hand, they are satisfied with good.

You hide Your face, they are dismayed; You take away their spirit, they expire And return to their dust.

You send forth Your Spirit, they are created; And You renew the face of the ground. (Psalm 104:24-30)

I find it easy to recognize the beauty and goodness of God in His creation. It is harder to remember that I am His beautiful creation too, and to see my place of dependence alongside the rest of creation.

Our culture celebrates independence, and I'm rather fond of it. I do not enjoy feeling needy or dependent, so I often find myself fighting God for independence, like a stubborn 3 year old determined to "do it myself!"

They all wait for You To give them their food in due season. You give to them, they gather it up; You open Your hand, they are satisfied with good.

What if dependence is not a curse, but a gift? Could I receive every need I have as an invitation back into my place as a creature, waiting for God to "open His hand"?

Could I make a practice of opening my hands to Him, in expectant hope that I would be satisfied with good?

What a high and holy view of God, our creator: He waits

14

for us to open our hands to Him, so He can open His hands to us.

> "Just as this is the very place and nature of God, to be unceasingly the supplier of every want in the creature, so the very place and nature of the creature is nothing but this – to wait upon God and receive from Him what He alone can give, what He delights to give." (Andrew Murray, Waiting on God.)

Lord Jesus, we ask for an open handed Advent, worshipping and waiting on you, our open handed God. We bow in dependence, submitting to our position as created beings, waiting on what You alone can give.

Journaling Prompts

Is the idea of depending on God encouraging to you, or does it seem hard and scary? Why?

What in your life makes you feel needy or dependent right now?

Write a prayer of dependence, submitting to God as your Creator and Provider, and expressing your trust in Him to provide. As you pray, picture yourself like the animals in Psalm 104, opening your hands and trusting God to satisfy you.

Waiting on God to Get What We Need

December 4

The Lord sustains all who fall and raises up all who are bowed down. The eyes of all look to You, And You give them their food in due time. (Psalm 145:14-15)

The King James version of Psalm 145:15 says "The eyes of all wait upon you...", making it a rephrasing of yesterday's truth.

But while Psalm 104 presents waiting as our place of dependence as creatures within nature, Psalm 145 presents waiting on God to provide, to give us what we need, as humanity.

Psalm 145 also gives us a beautiful synonym for waiting on God: "*the eyes of all look to You...*"

When you are in need, when you have a request or desire, a longing or a lack, where do you look?

Our needs and longings force us to look around, and we can practice looking up, to the source of life and goodness. But we must be willing to recognize our need, to acknowledge our lack, to wait. It is all too easy to numb, to escape, to ignore every hard emotion, the very emptiness that could put us on the path to satisfaction.

This advent, let's practice the art of noticing. Notice the lack, notice the need. Notice where you, where those you love, where this hurting world is bowed down and broken. And sit with those needs before a God who has promised to provide what we need.

Psalm 145

Great is the Lord, and highly to be praised, And His greatness is unsearchable. One generation shall praise Your works to another, And shall declare Your mighty acts. On the glorious splendor of Your majesty And on Your wonderful works, I will meditate.

Men shall speak of the power of Your awesome acts, And I will tell of Your greatness. They shall eagerly utter the memory of Your abundant goodness And will shout joyfully of Your righteousness.

The Lord is gracious and merciful; Slow to anger and great in lovingkindness. The Lord is good to all, And His mercies are over all His works.

All Your works shall give thanks to You, O Lord, and Your godly ones shall bless You. They shall speak of the glory of Your kingdom And talk of Your power; To make

17

known to the sons of men Your mighty acts and the glory of the majesty of Your kingdom. Your kingdom is an everlasting kingdom, and Your dominion endures throughout all generations.

The Lord sustains all who fall and raises up all who are bowed down. The eyes of all look to You, and You give them their food in due time. You open Your hand and satisfy the desire of every living thing.

The Lord is righteous in all His ways and kind in all His deeds. The Lord is near to all who call upon Him, to all who call upon Him in truth. He will fulfill the desire of those who fear Him; He will also hear their cry and will save them.

The Lord keeps all who love Him, But all wickedness He will destroy. My mouth will speak the praise of the Lord, and all flesh will bless His holy name forever and ever.

Journaling Prompts:

What needs in your life, your family, your community, feel heavy right now? How could you practice "looking to the Lord" in those heavy needs?

"One generation shall praise Your works to another, and shall declare Your mighty acts." (Psalm 145:4) How could you praise God's work to another generation this Advent? If you have children in your life, have you shared your story of God's faithfulness to you with them?

Take a few moments to meditate on the goodness of God in your life. Make a list of His goodness, specifically to you. How have you personally experienced the majesty and wonder of God your Father? How has He provided for you in the past?

Wait on God: You Will Not Be Disappointed

December 5

To You, O Lord, I lift up my soul. O my God, in You I trust,
Do not let me be ashamed; Do not let my enemies exult
over me. Indeed, none of those who wait for You will be
ashamed; Those who deal treacherously without cause
will be ashamed. Make me know Your ways, O Lord;
Teach me Your paths. Lead me in Your truth and teach
me, For You are the God of my salvation; For You I wait
all the day. (Psalm 25:1-5)

A long time ago, I began to pray for a life that could only
be explained by God. I want a life that requires faith. But
every time the Lord leads me to actual steps of faith I get
scared. I am scared of shame, scared of disappointment,
scared of failure. I've built my entire life on the belief in

the presence and goodness of God right here on earth. My hope in His nearness, my confidence in His Word, my assurance of His love guides my decisions and gives me purpose.

And I am still afraid.

I would like to continue to choose the Jesus Way. I want to let His character shape my spending, my giving, my time, my willingness to sacrifice. I want His character to shape me, even if it makes me appear foolish in the eyes of the world (and the church.) I want to live for the unseen, not just what I can see and touch and store up. This is the life I want, the life I've chosen. But it opens the door to doubt.

Will I regret these decisions, values, choices? Do they really matter?

What if this is all a lie, and there is no purpose to our lives? What if I've made the choices I believed were right, and it turns out I was wrong? What if none of this matters?

What if God isn't who I think He is?

The Psalmist cries out *"Do not let me be ashamed; Do not let my enemies exult over me."* And I receive with relief the promise of Psalm 25, *"None of those who wait for You will be ashamed."*

As I look back over my life so far, have I ever regretted trusting God?

No.

So I'll carry on, in the hope that I won't regret trusting Him today. I will keep lifting my soul to God. I will wait on God, even if I feel foolish. I will wait, even in the face of doubt and fear.

And I'll pray:

Make me know Your ways, O Lord; Teach me Your paths.
Lead me in Your truth and teach me, for You are the
God of my salvation;
For You I wait all the day.

(Psalm 25:4-5)

Journaling Prompts:

Doubt can be a great source of shame for Christians. But doubt is not the opposite of faith. And God isn't afraid of our doubts and fears. Take the power out of your doubts and fears by naming them before God. Tell Him the areas where you are afraid you'll be ashamed.

Have you ever regretted or been disappointed as a result of trusting God? How does this affect your ability to trust Him in the future?

Waiting on God in Psalm 25 is linked with knowing and living His Way. What in your life doesn't line up with God's ways?

Waiting on God With Strong Courage

December 6

Wait for the Lord; Be strong and let your heart take courage;
Yes, wait for the Lord. (Psalm 27:14)

I am not very strong, and I rarely feel brave. But Psalm 27 makes it seem like strength and courage are available to me, things I can choose.

The Message interprets Psalm 27:14: *Stay with God! Take heart. Don't quit. I'll say it again: Stay with God.*

I rarely feel strong or brave, but I do want to stay with God. I don't want to quit.

Psalm 27 contrasts waiting on God with listening to fear. In this context, strength is the refusal to listen to or be driven by fear.

The Lord is my light and my salvation; Whom shall I fear?
The Lord is the defense of my life; Whom shall I dread?
When evildoers came upon me to devour my flesh, My
adversaries and my enemies, they stumbled and fell.
Though a host encamp against me, My heart will not
fear; Though war arise against me, In spite of this I shall
be confident. (Psalm 27:1-3)

Here is my source of strength and bravery: What
darkness can touch me if God Himself is my light? What is
there to be afraid of if God Himself is my defender?

My problem (and yours too, I'd bet) is that when darkness
comes, I look for light on my own. I have all sorts of
refuges and places I run for safety before I go to God.

I am quick to think I need to defend myself.

This ancient prayer calls to us across the centuries,
reminding us that God is our safe place, our refuge, our
light, our defender. Psalm 27 teaches us that waiting on
God means choosing to see Him as bigger than our
circumstances, choosing not to give up, choosing to keep
seeking God and His goodness right here in our every
day lives.

Hear, O Lord, when I cry with my voice, And be gracious
to me and answer me. When You said, "Seek My face,"
my heart said to You, "Your face, O Lord, I shall seek."
(Psalm 27:7-8)

Are you in season of darkness, maybe even danger?

What would it look like for you to seek God's face, right in your circumstances?

Do you believe that He wants a face to face relationship with you?

Do you hear Him calling you, inviting you, this Advent season? Calling you to be strong, calling you to be brave? Calling you to hope?

> *I would have despaired unless I had believed that I would see the goodness of the Lord In the land of the living. Wait for the Lord; Be strong and let your heart take courage; Yes, wait for the Lord. (Psalm 27:13-14)*

Journaling Prompts:

What in your life right now requires you to choose to be strong and let your heart take courage? What makes you afraid?

What does it mean for you, personally, to seek God's face? What specifically are you doing to seek God this advent season?

As Christians, we are quick to believe we will experience the goodness of God in eternal life, but forget the promise of God's goodness in the here and now. Make a list of God's goodness to you here, in the land of the living.

Waiting on God: Conversations

December 7

Take a moment. Sit back, take a deep breath, stay for a moment in the stillness.

Ask God what it means for YOU to wait on Him.

Journal about what you're learning, listing any questions our study is stirring up for you, any encouragement you'd like to remember.

Go back and read any days you've missed, or answer any journaling questions that you didn't have time for.

Host a conversation

I often wonder how much deeper our relationships would be if we felt more comfortable talking about life and God openly with one another. With that in mind, talk about what you're learning this advent season with the people in your life.

Have these conversations over lunch after church on Sundays, as you grab coffee with friends, or as you gather around the dinner table. Don't put pressure on yourself with agendas or goals. Just ask your people what they think, and share what you're learning and thinking about.

Advent Conversation Starters:

What do you think it means to wait on God?

Isn't it is funny that we sing Silent Night during the Christmas season, when everything tends to be so loud? I've read that our souls need silence. Do you think you get as much silence as you need, or too much? Why?

On the first Sunday of Advent, churches and families light a candle symbolizing HOPE. What does the word hope mean to you? What feels hopeful in your life right now?

"Truly my soul waits upon God; from Him comes my salvation.'

First we wait on God for salvation. Then we learn that salvation is only to bring us to God and teach us to wait on Him. Then we find what is better still, that waiting on God is itself the highest salvation.

{Waiting on God} is ascribing to him the glory of being All. It is the experiencing that He is All to us.

May God teach us the blessedness of waiting on Him."

Andrew Murray, Waiting on God, 1968

Waiting on God: Our Hope is in Him

December 8

What is your favorite childhood Christmas memory? Mine is from sometime early in the 1980s, the year my sister and I asked for a Barbie Townhouse.

We knew it was expensive, so Santa Claus was our only hope. Khymberly and I shared a room back then, and always on Christmas Eve. I don't remember who woke whom up (probably me, she's always slept like the dead). But I do remember a whispered conversation, and the feeling of anticipation and hope. Knowing how much trouble we'd get in if we woke my parents up. Tiptoeing down the dark hallway, feeling our way across the living room to the Christmas Tree. The thrill as our hands found three stories of plastic goodness, knowing without seeing that it was bright pink. We sat in the dark, silently pulling the string to make the elevator go up and down. Our

29

hopes had been answered, and we silently celebrated as we crept back to our room and waited for the sun to rise.

My grown up Christmas hopes are more complicated, less able to be answered by anything you can stick a bow on. My grown up self knows the sting of disappointment, the chaos of a broken world. We wake up every day to bad news getting worse. It's hard to imagine anything sparking the childish anticipation and hope that found two little girls under a dark Christmas tree so long ago.

Where do we find hope in our grown up Christmases, which can sometimes be much darker than we imagined?

Hope is scary for me, because I am afraid of being disappointed. My hopes are bigger and weightier than Barbie Townhouses these days, so I am tempted to ignore them. I deny what I want, keep my dreams and desires reasonable, don't want to ask for too much. Do you relate?

Behold, the eye of the Lord is on those who fear Him, On those who hope for His lovingkindness,

To deliver their soul from death and to keep them alive in famine... (Psalm 33:18-19)

Look up, friend. The eye of the Lord is on you. He sees you, wherever this Christmas season finds you. Do you believe that He wants to delight you, even in the dark?

Watch this: God's eye is on those who respect him, the ones who are looking for his love.

He's ready to come to their rescue in bad times; in lean times he keeps body and soul together... (The Message)

This is good news: We have a God who is worth waiting on, who is ready and waiting for us. We look up to find His eyes on us.

When you wake in the night, rather than let your mind run to worries, fears, concerns, perhaps you can preach this promise to yourself?

Our soul waits for the Lord; He is our help and our shield.

For our heart rejoices in Him, because we trust in His holy name.

Let Your lovingkindness, O Lord, be upon us,

According as we have hoped in You. (Psalm 33:18-22)

Journaling Prompts:

What would it look like for you to look for God's love this Advent season? What does "looking for God's love" mean to you?

If you could ask God for anything this Christmas, for what would you ask Him?

Is it hard for you to ask God for what you want, to name what you hope for from Him? Why or why not?

Waiting Patiently on God

December 9

Rest in the Lord and wait patiently for Him... Psalm 37:7

Does patience come easily to you, or is waiting a struggle?

My patience is subjective and situational. Now that my daily life doesn't involve 3 year olds who insist on doing everything themselves, I find it easy to wait on a toddler who wants to zip her own jacket. I choose to be patient with kids (most of the time) when they're acting their age. And I try to practice patience when waiting in line, driving in traffic, all the normal patience-testing parts of being alive.

But I am not so patient with myself. I get frustrated and discouraged to struggle with the same issues year after year. I know I'm growing and changing, but it's so much easier to see how far I have to go, rather than how far I've come.

And it's never actually occurred to me that I need to be patient with God. But that is the command in Psalm 37: Wait patiently on the Lord.

The instruction to rest in the Lord and wait patiently on Him sounds passive to me. But the psalmist isn't telling us to sit out and do nothing. The Hebrew words translated here are *active* words. The word for rest means to be silent and still. But the word translated "wait patiently" has child-birth undertones: travailing, bringing forth. Birthing is definitely *not* a passive image of waiting.

What are you waiting on God *for*? Are you waiting patiently?

This makes me consider the things that make me anxious: Things I'd like to manage or control, outcomes I'd like guaranteed. I think about the unknowns in my future, about the uncertainties in my present. I think about advent and the kind of Christmas season I'd prefer to have (but may not even be a reasonable expectation, given my family and circumstances.)

In those things, what would it look like for me to be still and silent before God? In those things, what would it look like for me to wait patiently on God to work, like a mother bearing down as she gives birth?

I don't necessarily like my answers to these questions, and

I don't love the idea that waiting on God is like childbirth. Because birth involves pain, and silence doesn't come easily to me.

However.

If I really believe that what God is doing in my life is good... If I believe in His presence and goodness, if I believe the outcome of my waiting is new life, joy, relationship, love.... If I trust that God is birthing something beautiful, can I choose to wait patiently?

The people of Israel waited for generations for the promise of the Messiah to show up in the person of Jesus. Are we willing to wait?

Open up before, keep nothing back; He'll do whatever needs to be done: He'll validate your life in the clear light of day and stamp you with approval at high noon. Quiet down before, be prayerful before him. (Psalm 37:5-7, The Message)

Journaling Prompts:

How do you respond to the idea of patience as work, active waiting, like childbirth? Is this helpful imagery, or hard to get your mind around? Why?

What are you waiting on God *for*? Is it easy or hard for you to be patient in this waiting? Why?

What in God's character and your history with Him helps you to wait patiently on Him?

Waiting on God by Keeping His Ways

December 10

Wait for the Lord and keep His way, and He will exalt you... Psalm 37:34

Waiting on God is a posture. It involves my attitude, my disposition, my mindset. Waiting on God is something I do with my heart and mind. But Psalm 37:34 links my mindset with my actions.

"Wait passionately for God, don't leave the path." (The Message)

With my heart and mind I wait on God. With my body, my decisions, my will, I keep God's ways.

What does keeping God's way mean to you? For me, God's way is the Jesus way. The path I don't want to leave is the path of following Jesus.

Ironically, the Christmas season is the time of year when I experience the most dissonance between my way of life and the Jesus way.

I want Christmas to be about Jesus. I want to celebrate the birth of God-with-us in a stable, to a teenage peasant, in a backwater town. Jesus, who said,

> "The foxes have holes and the birds of the air have nests, but the Son of Man has nowhere to lay His head."
> (Matthew 8:20)

Jesus, whom Isaiah tells us had

> "no stately form or majesty That we should look upon Him, Nor appearance that we should be attracted to Him...." (Isaiah 53:2)

But my culture tells me I need to celebrate by:
- Giving those who have more than enough...more
- Asking for gifts, even when I already have more than I need
- Decorating my home, perhaps for the enjoyment of those who live and visit there, perhaps to impress the world via social media.
- Buying new clothes to wear to church on Christmas Eve.

What do we do with this contrast between the way we celebrate the birth of Jesus and how He lived His life?

These cultural expectations are embedded in our families

and traditions, they feel inescapable. And Ecclesiastes teaches us that... *"There is an appointed time for everything. And there is a time for every event under heaven...A time to mourn and a time to dance."* Surely there is no better reason to dance and celebrate than the nearness of God we remember at Christmas time.

So strike up the carols, deck the halls, cover everything in twinkle lights, do whatever it means to you to celebrate the birth of Jesus.

But perhaps we could also take some time in this Advent waiting, the time leading up to Christmas, to consider Jesus' ways. Let's think about the heart of God, what He loves, what He values.

How can we keep His ways this Advent season? What would He would consider the best Christmas gift?

Journaling Prompts:

What are some of the differences between how Jesus lived His life, and how you celebrate His birth? What is the Spirit saying to you about this contrast?

How might you wait on God by keeping His ways in your heart and mind this Christmas season?

How might you wait on God by keeping His ways in your habits, actions, spending, and giving this Christmas season?

Waiting on God For More Than We Know

December 11

And now, Lord, for what do I wait? My hope is in You.
(Psalm 39:7)

I am a question asker. I always have questions, and I sure like getting answers.

My early relationship with Jesus was driven by my questions, and I felt so secure and certain when answers were handed to me. For a while I had a well constructed theology, and I was motivated to tie up every loose end and rule out every contradiction. I was very sure about God's love and goodness, but my certainty was wrapped up in having all the right answers. It felt good to be certain.

Then life happened. And happened some more. Hard,

unexplainable, "where is God in this" moments began to poke holes in my certain answers. Life forced me into a corner with questions for which there are no answers.

I began to wonder if there was room in my theology for bigger questions, questions that might not have answers. Could I say, "I don't know", or "I'm not sure", but still be certain about God's love and goodness?

And I began to ask if my trust in God should be based on my ability to answer every question about Him... or on something bigger, more robust?

I began to stop chasing answers about God, and begin chasing God Himself.

Is there room in our waiting on God for mystery? Is there room in our advent for the unknown?

So often when we think about waiting on the Lord, we are waiting for something specific. When I pray and ask God about a situation in my life or someone else's, I usually have a pretty strong opinion about what He should do. I think I know exactly what answered prayer should look like. I think I know the best outcome.

Can I wait on God for I-don't-even-know-what?

Can I release my opinions on what He should do? Can I let go of my ideas of the best outcome? Can I open up my prayer to mystery and the unknown, and simply say, "My hope is in you"?

Might there be a part of our souls that stretches and grows, that feels welcomed to come out into the light, only when we admit that we're waiting on God for what we don't know?

Can we release ourselves from waiting on God to do what we want, and simply wait on Him?

Is there room in our waiting on God for mystery? Is there room in our advent for the unknown?

And now, Lord, for what do I wait? My hope is in You.
(Psalm 39:7)

Journaling Prompts:

How do you feel about mystery, the unknown? How does answering questions about God with "I don't know" make you feel?

Write about a time when life faced you with questions for which there are no easy answers. Talk to God about what this was like for you.

Think of an area of your life in which you are waiting on God, where you have a specific outcome or answer you're hoping for. Write out a prayer releasing that answer or outcome, moving to a place where your hope is not in the outcome you want, but in God Himself.

Waiting on God For a New Song

December 12

In my mid-20s, I found myself in a deep spiritual slump. I had been driven for so long by finding answers to my many questions. Once I thought I had the answers, I lost all motivation and most of my joy. I moved from a relatively emotional connection with the Lord to dryness, apathy, I jut didn't care.

It was terrifying.

In one of their earliest albums, the Christian band Caedmon's Call had a song called "Close of Autumn," that ends with these words:

An awful lot of talking, I don't leave You much to say
You didn't ever leave me

And my greatest fear Was You'd leave me here
A long time back my feet, could touch the bottom

I listened to that album nearly non-stop the summer it came out, and never made it through "Close of Autumn" without crying. I didn't like where I was spiritually, and I was so scared that God would leave me there.

He did not.

Fast forward a few years. I'd moved onto listening to other albums non-stop and forgot completely about "Close of Autumn." I found relationship with God beyond my emotions and began to discover His goodness outside my questions and answers. I entered a season of renewal, new life, new hope.

Spiritually, I was in a good place.

A friend put on the newest Caedmon's Call album, with an updated version of "Close of Autumn." I heard the words, *"You didn't leave me...and my greatest fear was you'd leave me here..."*, and tears came again. This time because He didn't leave me there.

Of course He didn't leave me there. And I knew that He wouldn't leave me here either, even in the good, happy, content place I was. He won't leave me. Ever.

I waited patiently for the Lord; and He inclined to me and heard my cry. He brought me up out of the pit of destruction, out of the miry clay,
And He set my feet upon a rock making my footsteps firm. He put a new song in my mouth, a song of praise to our God; Many will see and fear and will trust in the Lord.
(Psalm 40:1-3)

I don't know where this advent season finds you. Maybe you are in a dry, thirsty place, desperate for reasons to hope. Maybe you are in a beautiful place, seeking the Lord and finding Him. Using the imagery from Psalm 40, maybe you are in the pit? Or Maybe you are freshly delivered, with clay still clinging to your clothes? Or perhaps you are standing firmly on the rock, ready to sing a song of praise?

Wherever you are in your story, do you believe that God will never leave you? Ask Him for a new song, a song of praise to your God.

Journaling Prompts:

How would you describe the spiritual season you are in right now? What song are you singing?

Do you relate to my fear that God would leave me where I was spiritually? How have you experienced this fear?

Wherever you find yourself this Christmas season, can you write a prayer of praise to your God? What reasons has He given you to trust Him?

Waiting Eagerly For God

December 13

I wait for the Lord, my soul does wait, And in His word do I hope. My soul waits for the Lord more than the watchmen for the morning; Indeed, more than the watchmen for the morning. (Psalm 130:5-6)

In ancient Israel, without the benefit of electric light, night was a dangerous time. The watchmen on the walls of a city would wait and watch eagerly for morning, longing for the light of dawn to bring safety and security to the city.

And the psalmist says he waits for the Lord even more eagerly than the watchmen wait for morning.

When we were engaged, I longed for the day when Matt & I would no longer be separated by so many miles.

44

My city, my name, my job, my whole life was about to change drastically and I was so ready.

Being pregnant, I loved feeling the life growing inside of me. We were expectant and anxious to meet our baby and see who he would grow to be.

Adoption was a long season of eager waiting as a family. It felt like an elephant gestation, with days, weeks, months full of paperwork and red tape. The weeks I spent in Uganda felt interminable, as if we would never complete our adoption, making this precious orphan a son forever.

I watched my oldest wait restlessly through his senior year of high school, anxious for graduation and college. Now he is dreaming and eagerly planning for what comes next. I want to slow down the clock, but I can tell he would hit fast forward if he could.

Think of your seasons of eager waiting. Think of the watchmen on the walls of ancient Israel, waiting anxiously for the light of morning.

Is that how you wait for the Lord?

The watchmen waited eagerly for morning because they needed the light for life and safety. We are often insulated from physical danger or need. And we tend to run from our spiritual, emotional, mental needs.

We numb and run and hide and escape. It is so much easier to binge watch, to eat or drink, to fill our lives with busy and noise, rather than face the pain or need in our hearts.

But what if that pain we're running away from is the doorway through which we'll meet God? What if the darkness we are ignoring might be intended to whet our appetites for the light of God's Word? What if the things we're numbing and running from could help us to eagerly wait for the Lord?

If we were to give ourselves room, time, space to face the needs in our heart, the darkness in the world, might it change the way we wait for the Lord?

I wait for the Lord, my soul does wait, And in His word do I hope.
My soul waits for the Lord more than the watchmen for the morning;
Indeed, more than the watchmen for the morning.
(Psalm 130:5-6)

Journaling Prompts:

What are some of your stories of eager waiting? For what have you waited the most anxiously?

Can you imagine wanting and waiting for God they way you've waiting eagerly for other things in your life? Why or why not?

What do you need they way watchmen on the walls of ancient Israel needed the light of day? What darkness are you waiting for God to lift in your life?

Waiting on God: Conversations

December 14

Take a moment again this week. Sit back, take a deep breath, stay for a moment in the stillness.

Ask God what it means for YOU to wait on Him.

Journal about what you're learning, listing any questions our study is stirring up for you, any encouragement you'd like to remember. Look back at what you wrote at the beginning of the month, what you wanted from your December and Advent season, from this time you've set aside to learn about waiting on God. Is there anything you can change to move in the direction of what you want out of our December and Advent?

Go back and read any days you've missed, or answer any journaling questions that you didn't have time for.

Host a conversation

Talk about what you're learning this advent season with the people in your life.

Have these conversations over lunch after church on Sundays, as you grab coffee with friends, or as you gather around the dinner table. Don't put pressure on yourself with agendas or goals. Just ask your people what they think, and share what you're learning and thinking about.

Advent Conversation Starters:

What is your favorite Christmas memory?

Is Christmas more or less meaningful to you now than it was when you were younger? Why?

Is there anything in your life right now that feels like a waiting room? What are you waiting for? How hard is it for you to wait?

On the second Sunday of Advent, churches and families light a candle symbolizing FAITH. What is the difference between hope and faith? Which is more important: The strength of our faith, or the object of our faith? Why?

"The whole duty and blessedness of waiting on God has its root in this: That He is such a blessed Being, full to overflowing of goodness and power and life and joy., that we, however wretched, cannot for any time come into contact with Him without that life and power secretly, silently beginning to enter into and bless us....

Come with all that is dark and cold in you into the sunshine of God's holy, omnipotent love, and sit and wait there with the one thought: Here I am, in the sunshine of His love... Oh, do trust Him fully. Wait on the Lord!"

- Andrew Murray, Waiting on God, 1968

Waiting on God to Defeat Death

December 15

*He will swallow up death for all time, And the
Lord God will wipe tears away from all faces, and He
will remove the reproach of His people from all the
earth; For the Lord has spoken.*

*And it will be said in that day, "Behold, this is our God
for whom we have waited that He might save us. This is
the Lord for whom we have waited; Let us rejoice and
be glad in His salvation." (Isaiah 25:8-9)*

Here is a promise worth celebrating this Christmas
season! Truth for today and hope for tomorrow.

I have several dear friends who are looking death in the
eyes this Christmas: A family who just shepherded their
dear father and grandfather into the arms of Jesus. A

precious mother who is fighting bravely for her life, another who is preparing to say goodbye. My life is full of survivors who are thankful to be alive, but know full well what it feels like to be handed terrible news. We sit among those for whom Christmas is a reminder of death, with loved ones missing from their tables and celebrations.

My own family is marked by death. Two of my children came to me through the death of their mothers. My husband is a widower. My sweet father-in-law went home to Jesus at the very end of last year, so we are just finishing our first year without him.

When none of us are guaranteed tomorrow, and death feels like our enemy, what are we waiting on God *for?*

Isaiah calls to us across the centuries, promising a Redeemer: A God of deliverance, a God of Salvation, who will remove the disgrace of sin and banish death, wiping tears from our faces. For those in grief, this promise feels very tender.

Take a moment to look at the baby in a Nativity, the "holy infant so tender and mild" who sleeps in heavenly peace. Think about the newborn King whom the herald angels sing, the babe who is placed "away in the manger".

That baby whom we sing and celebrate this Christmas is the God Isaiah promised, who would swallow up death for all time. In Jesus, God has removed the reproach of

His people, and prepared to wipe away all our tears of grief.

Isaiah 25:8-9 is an already-but-not-yet promise. God has come near, we have welcomed His light in our hearts. He has begun the process of swallowing death. But still we sit in shadow, sometimes with tears on our faces, waiting.

Each of our paths will eventually lead through the valley of the shadow. But we have a God who is worth waiting on, even in the shadow of death. We need not fear, because God-with-us is with us. And He has already won the victory.

It will be said in that day, "Behold, this is our God for whom we have waited that He might save us. This is the Lord for whom we have waited; Let us rejoice and be glad in His salvation."

Journaling Prompts:

How has death touched your life and changed your Christmas experience?

We sit in an in between time—God has come near, and yet we wait to receive the fullness of the promise in Isaiah 25:8-9. How does this waiting frustrate you?

How does the promise in Isaiah 25 encourage you? Write out a prayer of thanks for who God is revealed in today's verse, and claim that promise for your life.

Waiting on God Who Waits For Us

December 16

Therefore the Lord longs to be gracious to you, And therefore He waits on high to have compassion on you. For the Lord is a God of justice; How blessed are all those who long for Him. (Isaiah 30:18)

How does it change your thoughts and feelings about waiting on God to know that He waits on you? The Message translates this lovely truth:

But God's not finished. He's waiting around to be gracious to you.
He's gathering strength to show mercy to you.
God takes the time to do everything right--everything.
Those who wait around for him are the lucky ones.

The beauty in this truth about God--He waits for us! - is

even more beautiful when we consider it in the context of the chapter it finishes off.

Isaiah 30 opens with serious words: *"Woe to the rebellious children," declares the Lord, "Who execute a plan, but not Mine, And make an alliance, but not of My Spirit, in order to add sin to sin..."*

The beautiful promise of a God who waits on us comes right on the heels of the Holy One of Israel saying to His people

"In repentance and rest you will be saved, In quietness and trust is your strength."

But you were not willing, and you said, "No, for we will flee on horses," Therefore you shall flee! "And we will ride on swift horses," Therefore those who pursue you shall be swift... (Isaiah 30:15-16)

These words hit close to home. We hear the voice of God calling us to repentance and rest, quietness and trust. But each of us carries the tendency of our Hebrew forerunners, who preferred to look for rescue and hope in the defenses and protection of the world, rather than in their covenant God.

Their God waited for His rebellious children to be ready for His mercy, His grace. He waited for them to be willing to receive.

And our heavenly, gracious, compassionate Father waits

for us. He waits of us to turn from every other hope of salvation and strength. He waits for us to come to the end of our plans and agendas. He waits for us to long for Him. He waits for us to be willing to wait for Him. He waits for me. He waits for you.

We wait for God. To answer, to hear, to heal, to do what we want Him to do, to do what He's promised to do.

And He? He waits for us.

> *In repentance and rest you will be saved,*
> *In quietness and trust is your strength."*

Are you ready to receive?

Journaling Prompts:

How does knowing that God waits on you change your thoughts and attitude about waiting on Him?

The Israelites of Isaiah's day turned to horses and foreign alliances for safety and salvation, rather than trusting in their God. What are some of the things you turn to for strength and hope rather than quietly trusting God?

What will you do during this Advent season to pursue repentance and rest, quietness and trust? Write out a prayer asking God for what you need in this area, and thank Him for waiting for you to turn to Him and be willing to receive.

Waiting on God for Strength

December 17

...Those who wait for the Lord Will gain new strength;
They will mount up with wings like eagles, They will run
and not get tired, They will walk and not become weary.
(Isaiah 40:31)

Our advent wait is nearly over. In a few weeks we'll pack up the Christmas decorations, make new year's resolutions, and think about what we need to cut back on so that our pants can fit again.

Are you tired?

Maybe you're tired from the travel and busyness of this season. Perhaps you entered December already worn out. We seem to be in a time of one negative news cycle after another, maybe you've been tired all year?

Dear friend, will you receive God's promise today as a gift and breath of fresh air? *Those who wait for the Lord will gain new strength...they will walk and not become weary.*

Isaiah 40 is one of my favorite chapters of the Bible, every word worth a read. The chapter opens with the words, "Comfort, O comfort My people," says your God...." and continues with one beautiful picture of the Lord after another: He is a shepherd gathering His lambs to carry them close. He is big enough to hold the oceans in the cup of His hand. He sits as sovereign, high above he circle of the earth, above the authority of every oppressive empire. He created the stars and knows them all by name.

In your weariness today, who do you need God to be?

What picture of God helps you rise above, to rise up with wings like an eagle?

Do you not know? Have you not heard? The Everlasting God, the Lord, the Creator of the ends of the earth does not become weary or tired. His understanding is inscrutable. He gives strength to the weary, And to him who lacks might He increases power.

Though youths grow weary and tired, And vigorous young men stumble badly, Yet those who wait for the Lord will gain new strength; They will mount

up with wings like eagles, They will run and not get tired,
They will walk and not become weary. (Isaiah 40:28-31)

Friend, are you tired? Sit awhile with your God who
never grows weary of you.

He gives strength to the weary, and to her who lacks
might, He gives His power.

Journaling Prompts:

Spend some time today being honest with God about
what makes you tired. Write out the things you are tired
of: in your life, in your relationship with God, in yourself.

Which picture of God in Isaiah 40 resonates with you
and encourages you today? Why?

Do you believe the promise that "He gives strength to the
weary" could be true for you? Why or why not? Write
out a prayer asking God for the strength you need right
now.

Waiting on God Who Acts on Our Behalf

December 18

For from days of old they have not heard or perceived by ear, Nor has the eye seen a God besides You, Who acts in behalf of the one who waits for Him. (Isaiah 64:4)

God acts on behalf of those who wait for Him. I love this truth. Never was there any God like Him, who "works for those who wait for Him." (The Message)

Do you believe that as you learn to wait on God, He is working for you?

Isaiah 64 is a chapter about sin and judgment. It isn't very encouraging or Christmas-y at all.

But how angry you've been with us! We've sinned and

kept at it so long!
there any hope for us? Can we be saved?
We're all sin-infected, sin-contaminated. Our best efforts
are grease-stained rags.
We dry up like autumn leaves—sin-dried, we're blown off
by the wind.
No one prays to you or makes the effort to reach out to
you because you've turned away from us, left us to stew
in our sins. (Isaiah 64:5-7, The Message)

The truth that God acts on behalf of those who wait for Him is a beautiful truth. How much more beautiful is it when we realize that the waiting in this passage is confession. Honesty.

Not: We have obeyed and listened and earned the right for you to work for us, so we wait.

But: We have sinned and gone astray. All of us have become like one who is unclean. And still we wait.

We live in a world and culture that trains us to never admit when we are wrong, to refuse to own the consequences of our choices. So we refuse to confess. We build walls between ourselves and others, and walls between ourselves and God.

Across the centuries, Isaiah demonstrates that we can admit when we are wrong. We can even confess the sin of our nation and people, without feeling defensive.

Isaiah leads us in bowing to the consequences of refusing to call on God. Isaiah bows to God's right to judge us, knowing He will not condemn.

But now, O Lord, You are our Father, We are the clay, and You our potter; And all of us are the work of Your hand. (Isaiah 64:8)

Isaiah teaches us to wait on God by confessing our sin, rather than ignoring or running away from the truth about ourselves.

And Isiah reminds us that we wait on God in the sure hope that He is a God who—even as we confess our sin and unfaithfulness—acts on behalf of those who wait for Him.

From the beginning of time, no one ever imagined a God like Him.

Journaling Prompts:

How do you feel about God's right to judge His people? Is this a reassuring concept for you, or is it scary? Why?

Take some time to confess your sins. What is in your heart right now that keeps you from calling on God and taking ahold of Him?

How does it change your thoughts about waiting on God to include confession and honesty about sin?

Waiting on God for His Unfailing Love

December 19

Remember my affliction and my wandering, the wormwood and bitterness. Surely my soul remembers and is bowed down within me. This I recall to my mind, therefore I have hope: The Lord's lovingkindnesses indeed never cease, For His compassions never fail. They are new every morning; Great is Your faithfulness.

"The Lord is my portion," says my soul, "Therefore I have hope in Him." The Lord is good to those who wait for Him, to the person who seeks Him. It is good that he waits silently for the salvation of the Lord. (Lamentations 3:19-26)

Where has affliction or wandering touched your life? Has bitterness entered into your story at all?

We like to pretend that Christians are people who have it all together, as if believing Jesus were a magic pill that helps us escape from hardship or reasons to complain.

But we know that's a lie, right? Jesus told us, "In this world you *will* have trouble." Some level of affliction or bitterness is likely to be a part of each of our lives.

What do we do with that bitterness? How do we respond to the harder parts of our stories? I like to ignore mine, denial is a girl's best friend. I also like to feed my pain, and I am especially good at running away from it. But I've learned you can't outrun your pain. Like Jeremiah in our verses today, I find myself occasionally saying, "Surely my soul remembers and is bowed down within me."

Jeremiah remembers, and is weighed down by his pain. But he doesn't stay there, and I don't want to either. From Lamentations 3, we learn the beautiful spiritual practice of *remembering*.

The truth is: Some parts of our stories are bitter. For many of us, the bitterness can be overwhelming. But bitterness isn't our whole truth. There's always a deeper truth we can choose to remember.

This I recall to my mind, therefore I have hope: The Lord's lovingkindnesses indeed never cease, For His compassions never fail. They are new every morning; Great is Your faithfulness.

Every morning of every day you wake up to a new store

of God's compassion. His love for you is never ending. His mercy will never fail you.

Being a Christian is not a get-out-of-jail-free card, giving us a pass on affliction or bitterness. But we do have the promise that affliction and bitterness are not the end of our story. And we have God's loyal, merciful love, His great faithfulness made new for us every day.

""The Lord is my portion," says my soul, "Therefore I have hope in Him." The Lord is good to those who wait for Him, to the person who seeks Him. It is good that he waits silently for the salvation of the Lord. (Lamentations 3:19-26)

Does your past or present include affliction and bitterness? Even if this Advent finds you in a season of bitterness, will you wait on God's goodness?

Journaling Prompts:

How have affliction or bitterness entered your story? In what areas are you tempted to let your soul be bowed down within you?

What could you do to incorporate the spiritual practice of remembering into your habits? What truths about God might you regularly need to call to mind?

Write a love letter to God, thanking Him for His compassionate, faithful, never ending love.

Failure & Waiting on God

December 20

But as for me, I will watch expectantly for the Lord; I will wait for the God of my salvation. My God will hear me.

Do not rejoice over me, O my enemy. Though I fall I will rise; Though I dwell in darkness, the Lord is a light for me. (Micah 7:7-8)

The college ministry I used to work for hosts a retreat in Colorado every fall that is a mountaintop experience for many. Every year students experience the presence and goodness of God and are sure they'll never waver or doubt again. They renounce lies they've believed about God and themselves, and commit to fighting sin and bondage. They return home sure they will have nothing but freedom and success from that point on.

I know better—from my own experience and from watching this cycle go around year after year.

Some come crashing down from that mountaintop and give up on God and themselves, and won't try again for years. Others learn to trust God even in their failure, finding Him in the valleys as well as the mountain tops. This is a waiting on God we *need* to learn, and one we need to encourage one another in.

How do we learn to wait on God, when we've failed to keep our own commitments and promises?

Just asking that question makes me anxious. No one loves failure, but I've spent most of my life not even attempting anything where success was not guaranteed. I am desperately afraid of failure.

I don't want to wait on God in the midst of failure. I don't want to learn things the hard way. I don't want to have to trust God to pick me up because I don't want to fall in the first place.

I am happy to have a Savior, but I don't want to need Him.

Do you relate? Or do you believe the other side of that lie, that you need to deal with your own failure, fix it and make it better, and *then* you can begin trusting the Lord?

For both of us, Jesus is the answer. He frees us from the

fear of regret and failure (a fear that imprisons us). And He frees us from the condemnation failure stamps on us like a scarlet letter (a shame too heavy for us to carry.)

Think of your greatest areas of failure. Where are you most afraid to fall? Where do you bear the shame of falling in the past?

In those areas, will you watch expectantly for the Lord? He does hear you.

Do not rejoice over us, O our enemy. Though we fail and fall, by the grace of God WE WILL RISE.

Journaling Prompts:

Do you believe that moral or spiritual failure exempts you from the goodness of God? Why or why not?

How have you been tempted to give up on yourself and/or God in the face of failure?

How do you respond to failure? Do you promise yourself and God to do better next time? Do you make resolutions? What would it look like for you to trust God in the midst of failure?

Waiting on God: Conversations

December 21

This close to Christmas, you may have to fight for it, but try to take a few moments to be still today. Sit back, take a deep breath, stay for a moment in the quiet.

Ask God what it means for YOU to wait on Him.

Journal about what you're learning, write down any questions our study is stirring up for you, any encouragement you'd like to remember. Look back at what you wrote at the beginning of the month, what you wanted from your December and Advent season, from this time you've set aside to learn about waiting on God. **What could you do to connect with Jesus and slow down, these last days before Christmas?**

Go back and read any days you've missed, or answer any journaling questions that you didn't have time for.

Host a conversation

Talk about what you're learning this advent season with the people in your life.

Have these conversations over lunch after church, as you grab coffee with friends, or as you gather around the dinner table. Don't put pressure on yourself with agendas or goals. Just ask your people what they think, and share what you're learning and thinking about.

Advent Conversation Starters:

Are you afraid of dying? Why or why not?

When you feel like you've failed God, yourself, or someone else, how do you respond?

On the third Sunday of Advent, churches and families light the candle symbolizing JOY. Traditionally, the joy candle is pink. What color is joy to you? What are some things that bring joy into your life?

The giver is more than the gift.

God is more than the blessing; and our being kept waiting on Him is the only way for our learning to find our life and joy in Him. Oh, if God's children only knew what a glorious God they have, and what a privilege it is to be linked in fellowship with Him, then they would rejoice in Him, even when He keeps them waiting...

Let every thought of waiting become to us simply the expression of unmingled and unutterable blessedness, because it brings us to a God who waits that He may make Himself known to us perfectly as the Gracious One."

- Andrew Murray, Waiting on God, 1968

Waiting on God to Keep His Promises

December 22

*And there was a man in Jerusalem whose name was
Simeon; and this man was righteous and
devout, looking for the consolation of Israel; and the
Holy Spirit was upon him. And it had been revealed to
him by the Holy Spirit that he would not see death
before he had seen the Lord's Christ.*

*And he came in the Spirit into the temple; and when the
parents brought in the child Jesus, to carry out for Him
the custom of the Law, then he took Him into his arms,
and blessed God... (Luke 2:25-28)*

The time between the last prophecy of Malachi in the Old
Testament and the birth of Christ was 400 years, known
as the 400 years of silence. "The world in solemn stillness
lay..." Israel had all the promises of the coming Messiah
King, the nation had been returned to the land, but was
ruled by one foreign power after another. Israel waited.

The 400 years of silence was coming to a close, unknown to anyone except an old man named Simeon.

Simeon was "a man who lived in prayerful expectancy..." (The Message). He lived his life waiting for the promised Messiah. And as Mary and Joseph brought 8 day old Jesus to the temple for circumcision, Simeon knew his expectation had been answered. The day he waited for was at hand.

Our world practically worships youth, but we have so much to learn from older saints. What would it be like to receive a promise from God and wait until your old age to see it come to fruition? Are we willing to wait to see God keep His promises, even if we wait nearly until our death?

The New Testament book of Hebrews says of Old Testament followers of God "All these died in faith, without receiving the promises, but having seen them and having welcomed them from a distance..." (Hebrews 11: 13) Simeon lived to see the promise of God in the infant Jesus.

Right now in this Christmas season we celebrate the keeping of the promise for which Simeon and ancient Israel waited. We can say with Simeon this Advent,

"...My eyes have seen Your salvation, which You have prepared in the presence of all peoples, a Light of revelation to the Gentiles, and the glory of Your people Israel." (Luke 2:30-32)

We live in the fullness of Emmanuel, God-with-us, and the constant comfort of God's Spirit and presence with us. We have the blessing ancient Israel longed for, the promises for which Simeon waited and watched.

But we join Simeon and the saints of old, waiting on God to keep His promise of goodness in this fallen world. To be honest, I don't really want to wait until the end of my life to see God's goodness in some of the areas for which I pray. And I certainly don't want to die in faith, welcoming God's promise of goodness from afar.

But I will take Simeon as my teacher, and I will look to the Old Testament men and women of faith in Hebrews 11 to guide me. I will let the kept promises of Christmas encourage me, and I will believe God keeps all His promises. I will wait.

Journaling Prompts:

What is the longest you've waited and prayed for something? What prayers have you waited the longest to be answered?

What do you think about the prospect of waiting until the end of your life to see God's goodness or receive His specific promises to you? How do you feel about possibly entering death without seeing answered prayer in some areas? Be honest with God about how this makes you feel, and ask Him for endurance to keep waiting and trusting Him.

Waiting on God for the Return of His Son

December 23

"Be generous. Give to the poor. Get yourselves a bank that can't go bankrupt, a bank in heaven far from bank robbers, safe from embezzlers, a bank you can bank on. It's obvious, isn't it? The place where your treasure is, is the place you will most want to be, and end up being.

Keep your shirts on; keep the lights on! Be like house servants waiting for their master to come back from his honeymoon, awake and ready to open the door when he arrives and knocks. Lucky the servants whom the master finds on watch! He'll put on an apron, sit them at the table, and serve them a meal, sharing his wedding feast with them. It doesn't matter what time of the night he arrives; they're awake—and so blessed! (Luke 12:33-38, The Message)

We know that Jesus is the One for Whom the whole world waited, but the wait is not over. Because Advent both reflects the long wait for Jesus's first coming, and reminds His people that we wait for Him to come again.

The Second Coming of Christ is the focus of centuries of theological debate, about the when and the how. We're told specifically that no one will know the when, and the questions of how are way above my pay grade, but I do know two things:

Jesus' Second Coming, like His first, will reflect the character of the Father, Son, and Spirit, and is for the good of the world He created and everyone in it.

And we are to be ready.

He is coming to bring His Kingdom in fullness, so readiness begins with living His Kingdom values as we wait. As we celebrate the birth of Christ, I want to commit to studying the life of Christ and following His example.

What does it look like to live waiting for the return of God's Son? Each of us might answer that question differently, but we can look to the apostle Paul's instruction to Timothy as a guide:

> *But flee from these things, you (wo)man of God, and pursue righteousness, godliness, faith, love, perseverance and gentleness. Fight the good fight of faith; take hold of the eternal life to which you were called, and you made the good*

confession in the presence of many witnesses.

I charge you in the presence of God, who gives life to all things, and of Christ Jesus, who testified the good confession before Pontius Pilate, that you keep the commandment without stain or reproach until the appearing of our Lord Jesus Christ, which He will bring about at the proper time—He who is the blessed and only Sovereign, the King of kings and Lord of lords, who alone possesses immortality and dwells in unapproachable light, whom no man has seen or can see. To Him be honor and eternal dominion! Amen. 1 Timothy 6:11-16

Journaling Prompts:

What do you know about the second coming of Christ? Is this a scary, confusing, or comforting idea for you?

What did it look like for those living before the birth of Christ to be ready to receive the promised Messiah? What made people ready or not ready for Jesus during His life on earth?

What do we learn from Jesus' first coming (How Jesus came, what He was like and what He did), that might help us wait and prepare for His second coming?

Waiting on God Continually

December 24

Therefore, return to your God, observe kindness and justice, And wait for your God continually. (Hosea 12:6)

When I talk about waiting on God, I usually mean I'm waiting on God to do something. I'm waiting for Him to answer my prayer, to deliver a certain outcome, to keep a promise in His Word.

Studying the words of Scripture and learning the Biblical usage of "waiting on God" has stretched and expanded my definition. I'm learning to see waiting on God as a way of life, an attitude I cultivate. Waiting on God is a posture of my heart.

When I picture this posture, waiting on God isn't sitting back with my arms crossed. It isn't an impatient, tapping toe. A posture of waiting isn't a raised fist, a turned back, a downcast head.

I picture the posture of a waiting heart as a lifted face. Open hands. Bowed knees. Postures of expectant, hopeful trust.

I also see this posture overflowing from my responses to God into my responses to others.

Can I wait on God in expectant hope, and then turn my back on my brother? Can I wait on God's goodness with open hands, and then raise my fist to those created in His image?

And does this posture, does my waiting have an expiration date? Am I committed to waiting on God expectantly, and opening my hands to my fellow man, only for a certain amount of time?

... Wait for your God continually.

Waiting on God in expectant hope, looking to Him, bowing my knees and opening my hands to Him and to others is not a posture that comes naturally to me. This is a posture, a heart attitude that needs to be cultivated.

I will not wait for my God continually by accident.

I wait for God continually as I continually look for His beauty and goodness in the world around me. I wait for God continually as I gather with other believers and God-seekers, to celebrate His grace and goodness. I wait for

God continually by daily seeking stillness, by looking for His character and goodness in His Word and in my story. I wait for God continually as I say yes to Him, moment by moment, day by day. This is the posture I want to carry out of advent, into the new year.

Joy to the World, the Lord has come. This is our God, for whom we wait, continually.

Journaling Prompts:

If you picture waiting on God as a posture of your heart, what body posture do you picture? Which posture resonates the most with you, as a picture of waiting on God continually?

What is the Spirit whispering to you about your posture toward God? What attitudes might you need to cultivate in order to wait on God continually?

How should our posture toward God be reflected in our posture toward others? What is the Spirit saying about this to you? What attitude toward others might you need to cultivate in order to wait on God in integrity?

Waiting on God Only

December 25

My soul, wait in silence for God only, For my hope is from Him. He only is my rock and my salvation... (Psalm 62:5-6)

Merry Christmas!

We're finishing where we started, saying to our souls with Psalm 62: *Wait in silence for God only.*

I've been interested in the concept of waiting on God for over a decade. I first read Andrew Murray's book on Waiting on God at least 20 years ago, and I've lost track of how many times I've read it since.

Many of the verses we've considered this month are among my all-time favorites, life verses that greet me like old friends.

I've let these verses and the psalmists and prophets who wrote them tutor me in waiting on God, and I can say with gratitude that I have grown in many aspects of waiting on God.

I am not an expert, but I do have experience turning my face to God, and shaping the posture of my heart around waiting on God continually.

But when it comes to waiting on God *only* I still feel like a beginner, I'm just scratching the surface.

My soul feels sticky, like it has a magnetic attraction to waiting on other things. Not always instead of God these days, but along with God. I'm waiting on God, but I'm also waiting on lots of other things I think I need in order to be safe, valued, or happy.

I trust God. But if I'm honest, what I really mean is "I trust God and..."

God and everything on my Christmas list, God and being able to give my family everything on their lists. God and a healthy body. God and my family. God and a comfortable home and all that I need physically. God and a job, a steady income, a known future, a padded bank account. God and good friends, a safe community, a stable city, state, country.

If you mess with any of those things, waiting on God in trust and hope becomes much more difficult.

But God *is* enough. He alone is my safety and security,

He alone is my hope. This is the promise of Christmas: Emmanuel, God with us. Even if all of my "God and..." things are lost, stripped from me, God is WITH me.

And He is with you. By God's grace we can embrace the Christmas miracle, release our "God and..." hopes, and tell our souls: *My soul, in silence for God only...*

> *O holy Child of Bethlehem descend to us, we pray*
> *Cast out our sin and enter in, be born to us today*
> *We hear the Christmas angels the great glad tidings tell:*
> *O come to us, abide with us, Our Lord Emmanuel*

> *(O Little Town of Bethlehem)*

Journaling Prompts:

God is your hope, you will not be disappointed as you wait on Him, only. What have you learned about waiting on God over this Advent season?

Find some time today to thank God. Write a prayer of thanks for who Jesus is to you this Christmas, and ask for His grace to continue learning to wait on Him only.

Happy New Year

I am so grateful for our time together through this Advent Season.

I hope our 25 days together pointed you in some small way toward the goodness of our God. And I hope you've found, like I have, that you may already have much of the goodness you are waiting for, because you have Him.

The journey doesn't have to end here. My favorite day of the year is New Year's Day. I love resolutions and goals, and I love the idea of a fresh new year. A new start.

New Year's Resolutions might feel arbitrary or burdensome, but the beginning of the year really can be a great time to start new habits. What could you do in the new year to help you continue to grow in waiting on God? Throughout our advent study, did you sense the Spirit calling you to something more or deeper with Him? I hope you'll say yes!

"At our first entrance into the school of waiting upon God, the heart is chiefly set upon the blessings which we wait for. God graciously uses our need and desire for help to educate us for something higher than we were thinking of. We were seeking gifts. He, the Giver, longs to give Himself and to satisfy the soul with His goodness... He is all the time seeking to win the heart of His child for Himself. He wishes that we should not only say, when He bestows the gift, How good is God! But that long before it comes, and even if it never comes, we should all the time be experiencing, 'The Lord is GOOD to them that wait for Him.'"

- Andrew Murray, Waiting on God, 1968

If you enjoyed this devotional, I would so appreciate it if you'd leave a review wherever you bought it. Reviews will help other readers find Waiting on God and hopefully go on their own Advent journey.

Come visit reemeyer.com where you'll find ways to contact me, along with occasional blog posts.

Looking for more Devotionals or Bible Studies for groups or individuals? Check out the free downloadable resources available on my website:

14 Days of Love

Spend a couple of weeks thinking about God's love, and asking how you can RECEIVE God's love and OFFER love to others. Designed to be used between February 1-14, but love works every month!

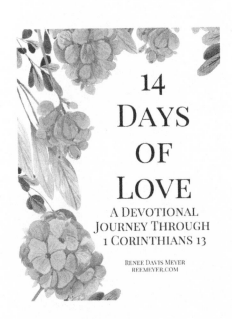

Do Not Fear: 14 Days of Devotional Reflections on the
Bible's Most Repeated Command

 So much in our lives tempts us to look at obstacles, at our
lack, at the things we fear. And God invites us to look to
Him, to look to love. How do you fight fear with the
knowledge of God's love? Fear has long been my biggest
enemy, and my current season of life has me facing fears
down left and right. I decided to dive deep into God's
counsel, the most repeated command in the Bible: Do
Not Fear.

The Last Words of Jesus: A Holy Week Devotional

This 7 day journey walks from Palm Sunday to Good
Friday, focusing on a phrase Jesus spoke from the cross
each day. Join me as we slow down and look closely at
Jesus on the Cross in the week before Easter.

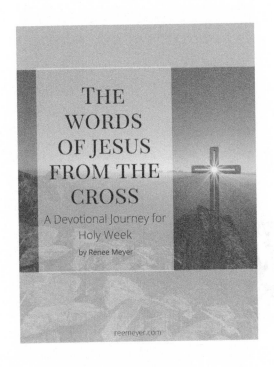

THE
WORDS
OF JESUS
FROM THE
CROSS
A Devotional Journey for
Holy Week
by Renee Meyer

reemeyer.com

Renee Davis Meyer is a writer, Bible teacher, and community builder located in Lincoln, NE (though she's a Texas girl at heart.) After years in college ministry, serving alongside her pastor husband, and writing and teaching Bible Studies for women, last year Renee joined a Lincoln nonprofit to run a children's ministry for underprivileged kids. Renee and Matt are parents to three boys, the oldest of whom is in college and getting married next year.

Renee's favorite thing about God is that He makes ugly things beautiful - He can take the hardest things this fallen world throws at us, and grow life and beauty. The circle of God's love is wider than you think it is, there is room for each of us.

Renee can be found:

WEBSITE reemeyer.com

INSTAGRAM Renee Davis Meyer

FACEBOOK Renee Davis Meyer

EMAIL reemeyerblog@gmail.com

Made in the USA
Monee, IL
21 November 2020